Dedicated to **Nancy Booher, my Mother-In-Law.**

Your life embodied the true meaning of unconditional **LOVE**. Your kindness, acceptance and dedication to your family, tore down walls, changed hearts and ensured, above all, that **LOVE** was given and experienced by everyone!

"Lights out Aidan,
it's now time to go to bed!"

"Tomorrow's the big day so rest your sleepy head."

"That's right Dad! I get to play
soccer with Isabel and Tim.
And then after we play,
we get to go and swim!"

"I like being friends with them
as we play all our games."

"But something is different,
our families are not the same."

"At Tim's, there's no daddy, he just has his mom.
Isabelle has two daddies and no mommy.
How come?

You could see on his face, Aidan was very confused,
but his mommy was certain, she knew just what to do.

"Yes, their families are different,
but we are all just the same.
Here's a little bedtime story and I will try to explain."

There was once a very nice hen,
Molly was her name.
She was always sweet and kind
and treated everyone the same.

She protected the chicks
from the rain with her wing,

and kept them safe from every little thing.

Then one night as she lay there,
just trying to get some rest,
she started laying eggs,
right there in her nest!

She jumped to her feet and much to her surprise,
there were seven beautiful eggs,
each a different color and size.

"Oh my! Oh dear! What have we here?"
"Seven precious eggs, so special and rare."

But her nest for these precious
eggs was just too small,
so she asked other hens
if they would help raise them all.

Some hens were too busy and some didn't care.
Some hens just laughed while others would stare.

Then through the barn doors
walked the wise Mother Hen.
She said, "I'll help you Molly and
I'll do the best that I can!"

Molly was so happy and she thanked Mother Hen.
Now her nest and her eggs would be warm in the pen.

There was red and orange,
there was purple and green,
yellow and pink and the bluest blue she'd ever seen.

"Oh my Molly!
What special rainbow eggs that I see."

"I'll keep them safe and warm and very close to me."

"I'll be back!" said Molly,
as she flew through the door,
in search of folks who wanted children for sure.

It was now breakfast time
and waiting outside of the barn,
Was a rooster and a chicken
who were new to the farm.

Molly went to ask them if they would like two special eggs.

They said "Yes!" right away
as they danced on their legs!

As she gave them the red and orange eggs,
she began to feel sad.
"Will I ever see them again?"
was the feeling she had.

But seeing the joy on their faces,
it made Molly see,
that with her precious eggs,
it would make them a family.

It was soon time for lunch
and as the chickens started to gather.
her friends, the two hens,
were laughing with each other.

Molly asked them if they would
like to have two special eggs.

They said "Yes!"
right away as they danced on their legs!

As she gave them the green and purple eggs
she began to feel sad.
"Will I ever see them again?"
was the feeling she had.

But seeing the joy on their faces,
it made Molly see,
that with her precious eggs,
it would make them a family.

It was soon time for dinner
and sitting way up in the shed,
were two strong roosters
who made sure everyone got fed.

Molly asked them if they would like
to have two special eggs.

They said "Yes!" right away
as they danced on their legs!

As she gave them the pink and yellow eggs
she began to feel sad.
"Will I ever see them again?"
was the feeling she had.

But seeing the joy on their faces,
it made Molly see,
that with her precious eggs,
it would make them a family.

As Molly raced back
to get the only egg that was left,
she was stopped by the hens
that didn't want to help.

They said, "We watched all day as you gave
your eggs to roosters and hens,
but we don't agree with two roosters
who are much more than friends!"

"You see, chicks need a hen
to raise them up right.
Not two roosters
who only know how to crow and fight!"

Then through the barn doors
walked the wise Mother Hen,
who said, "Don't worry Molly,
I'll take care of these silly hens!"

"It can be a mommy and daddy
that can make a family.
And with two mommies or two daddies,
a great family they can be!"

Mother Hen said to the hens,
"So you are very wrong!
Chicks need a loving home
where they're cared for and belong."

"Molly, it's soon time for bed
and now there's one egg, its blue."
This one too is special, so what are you going to do?"

She held her egg very close,
she would keep it, she would.
She wanted to keep them all,
but there was no way that she could.

The thought of giving away her eggs,
at first made her very sad.

But in their new families,
they have made someone a new mom or dad!

So Aidan, it takes a man and a woman
to make a baby, that may be,

but really, all you need is

LOVE

to make a family!

One Love Stories

Made in the USA
Lexington, KY
11 April 2018